Exodus From Belgium
in 1940

EXODUS FROM BELGIUM IN 1940

A Family's Escape To South America and
Final Emigration to the United States

PAUL BORNSTEIN

Library of Congress Control Number:		2012904179
ISBN:	Hardcover	978-1-4691-8000-7
	Softcover	978-1-4691-7999-5
	Ebook	978-1-4691-8001-4

This book was printed in the United States of America.

To order additional copies of this book, contact:
Xlibris Corporation
1-888-795-4274
www.Xlibris.com
Orders@Xlibris.com
111365

Contents

DEDICATION

To my parents, Abraham and Mina Bornstein, whose foresight, courage, and fortitude gave me the opportunity to write this book.

Chapter 1

Departure from Antwerp, May 1940

Invasion by Germany

WAS IT A thunderstorm or the bombing of the port of Antwerp by the Luftwaffe? I was less than six years old and was awakened by the noise and flashing lights caused by exploding bombs. My father calmed me by drawing the blinds shut and blamed the noise and lights on a thunderstorm. In reality, Germany had attacked Belgium without prior warning. This attack was part of a larger assault that included the invasion of Luxembourg and the Netherlands. The German army had broken through Belgian defenses in the Ardennes Forest, and was advancing westward, preceded by elements of the French and British armies, which were attempting to reach ports on the English Channel, such as Dunkirk, for evacuation to England.

Figure 1-1 My parents at a beach in Belgium, shortly after their marriage in 1933 (photographer unknown).

Figure 1-2 Paul and Viviane on the beach in Ostende, Belgium, 1938 (photographer unknown).

My father had apparently reached a similar decision. The next two days, a weekend, were spent making difficult decisions as to which items to stow in our De Soto Sedan, and which to leave behind. Our party consisted of my parents (fig. 1-1), my four-year-old sister, Viviane, and me (fig. 1-2) and my bachelor uncle, Henry. Priority was given to small valuable items, such as jewelry, that could be sold more easily, because money could not be withdrawn from banks over the weekend; in any case, the banks did not open due to the chaos caused by the bombardment. Valuable but bulky items, such as our piano, had to be left behind. However, my father did take some time to bury a few large pieces of silver in our backyard garden. When he returned to Antwerp after the war to determine whether he wished to return to Belgium and resume his medical practice (he did not), the silver was still there, and our house on Avenue de Belgique (fig. 1-3) was intact.

Figure 1-3 Our house on the Avenue de Belgique. The black gate on the left blocked a driveway that led to a garage and a large garden. The house extended to include the three windows on the right, plus a basement and an attic.

Figure 1-4 A 1936 De Soto, similar to the one we had. Note the running board. Photograph reproduced from www.connorsmotorcar. com 11/29/2010 1:36 PM, MST.

The De Soto Sedan

After completing his medical training in Brussels and recuperating from tuberculosis in Davos, Switzerland, my father had opened a practice in Antwerp. To serve his patients, he needed an automobile. After some searching, he noticed an advertisement for a late model De Soto Sedan at a local garage. A comparable image is shown in figure 1-4. My father was prepared to purchase the vehicle when the seller confided that it was equipped with a special feature. He had worked as a smuggler, transporting watches across the border from Switzerland to France. Customs officials attempted to detect such illicit trade by stepping vigorously on the bumpers of the vehicle and causing the watches to tick; with a stethoscope placed on various surfaces of the car, the watches were revealed by their telltale noise. To thwart such detection, the smuggler had built a relatively soundproof compartment into the car. For an additional sum of money, he was willing to reveal the location of the compartment. After some consideration, my father declined the offer. He reasoned that should he ever have a use for it, he could easily have a mechanic in the garage locate the compartment—a decision he was to regret later.

Our attempt to reach England via Dunkirk

After loading as much luggage as possible into our car, and with my uncle standing on the running board of the De Soto, we joined an increasing stream of both civilian and French and British military vehicles headed in the direction of Dunkirk. Progress was slow, due both to the volume of the traffic and the tendency of military vehicles to run civilian vehicles off the road if they hindered their progress. An even more serious problem was the presence of German fighter planes that strafed vehicles, regardless of whether they were civilian or military, in order to clog the roads and hinder access of British and French military personnel to ships waiting in Dunkirk to transport them to British ports. On several occasions, to avoid being strafed, my father, upon hearing the approach of the planes, left the main road and drove to a grassy patch, where he covered the car with a green tarpaulin to disguise its presence. Nevertheless, at some point, the decision was made to abandon our attempt to reach Dunkirk and to drive instead to the south of France, because it seemed unlikely at the time that the German invasion would reach there. This decision was supported by stories, circulating among refugees, that conditions at Dunkirk were chaotic (fig. 1-5) and that transport of nonmilitary refugees to England was far from assured.

Figure 1-5 Chaotic conditions at Dunkirk, May 1940. From http://
www.rania.co.uk/dunkirk/html/history.htm.

The decision is made to leave France by another route

I have little information regarding the route we took through France that led us to the small town of Cognac, a short distance from the port of Bordeaux. However, my father's initial intent was to drive to Paris, a city he considered safe at the time. A stroke of good fortune obliged him to stop in a small town to have a burnt wire in the car replaced. While speaking with the mechanic, my father was informed that the German army was closing in on Paris and was likely to be there before we could reach it. Had he continued on to Paris, I would most likely not be here to tell this story.

Presumably, Bordeaux was chosen as an alternative destination because it had a substantial port that might have nautical traffic to England. It seems difficult to believe that Uncle Henry was able to stand on the running board of the De Soto for the entire distance, which could have been as long as several hundred miles. Fortunately, in Bordeaux, we were told that, indeed, ships left from time to time for destinations in England. Accordingly, we rented rooms on a farm in the nearby town of Cognac. My most vivid memory of the time we spent at the farm resulted from the task I was given, namely, to collect the eggs laid by chickens that wandered around the grounds. My father and uncle traveled frequently to Bordeaux, for news of a ship destined to travel to England. After some weeks, one materialized, but we were informed, to our dismay, that passage was limited to passengers with a British passport. My uncle, together with other members of the family including my father, had left Belgium for England during World War I. Toward the end of the war, Uncle Henry had joined the British army and had thereby received a British passport. Because there seemed to be no possibility for the rest of us to obtain passage to England, we left Bordeaux and made our way to the French-Spanish border. What followed was a quirk of fate that troubled my parents, and later my sister and me, for many years to come. Shortly after leaving Bordeaux, my uncle was informed by the ship's captain that close relatives of passengers with a British passport were now also eligible for travel to England. Since Henry knew the route we planned to take to Spain, he immediately rented a taxi in an unsuccessful attempt to overtake us. In later years, I, and I imagine my parents and sister as well, must have wondered which paths our lives would have taken had we gone to England instead of British Guiana (now known as Guyana), and later to the United States.

A rapid traverse through Spain and Portugal to the port city of Lisbon, and onward to New York

We had been warned in France that Spanish border guards were prone to confiscate jewelry and other precious items on grounds that special permits were required to import them into the country. As we prepared to cross the border, my father rued the day that he turned down the opportunity to learn the location of the special compartment in his De Soto that the smuggler had used to hide his watches as he crossed the Swiss-French border. As an alternative, he cached my mother's jewelry in a large floppy cloth doll from which my sister was inseparable. The ruse was successful and the jewelry proved to be essential for paying our expenses until we reached British Guiana.

We drove through Spain and Portugal as quickly as possible to catch the first available ship leaving Lisbon. Upon arrival in Lisbon, my father contacted the consul of the United States who provided him with a passport visa, dated August 7, 1940, which gave our family permission to transit the United States on our way to British Guiana (fig. 1-6).

I am aware that my entry into the United States is subject to the immigration laws of the United States, including the act of February 5, 1917, section 3 of which provides for the exclusion of aliens of various classes, and the act of October 16, 1918, which, as amended by the act of June 5, 1920, provides for the exclusion of anarchists, and other persons who hold to or support doctrines or movements of a politically subversive character, inimical to the United States, directly or through membership in, or affiliation with, organizations of a subversive character.

I realize that if I am found to be one of a class inadmissible into the United States under any of the provisions of the immigration laws of the United States, or if my classification as a nonimmigrant alien is not approved upon arrival in the United States, I may be detained, or excluded and deported, by the immigration authorities, and I am prepared to assume the risks of such detention, or exclusion and deportation.

I understand that section 15 of the Immigration Act of 1924 provides that: "The admission to the United States of an alien excepted from the class of immigrants * * * shall be for such time as may be by regulations prescribed, and under such conditions as may be by regulations prescribed (including, when deemed necessary for the classes mentioned in clause (2), (3), (4), or (6) of section 3 * * * the giving of bond with sufficient surety, in such sum and containing such conditions as may be by regulations prescribed) to insure that, at the expiration of such time or upon failure to maintain the status under which admitted, he will depart from the United States."

I am aware that section 2 of the Deportation Act of March 4, 1929, as amended, provides that: "Any alien who hereafter enters the United States at any time or place other than as designated by immigration officials or eludes examination or inspection by immigration officials, or obtains entry to the United States by a willfully false or misleading representation or the willful concealment of a material fact, shall be guilty of a misdemeanor and, upon conviction, shall be punished by imprisonment for not more than 1 year or by a fine of not more than $1,000, or by both such fine and imprisonment."

I realize that section 22 (c) of the Immigration Act of 1924 provides that: "Whoever knowingly makes under oath any false statement in any application, affidavit, or other document required by the immigration laws or regulations prescribed thereunder, shall, upon conviction thereof, be fined not more than $10,000, or imprisoned for not more than 5 years, or both."

I solemnly swear that the foregoing statements are true to the best of my knowledge and belief. and I understand that I shall be obliged to depart from the United States at the end of my temporary sojourn.

H. G. Hoynman
(Signature of applicant, with at least one Christian name)

Subscribed and sworn to before me this ....7th........ day of ....August........, 19.40..

[SEAL]

Fee No. ....2678....

Passport visa No. ....173....

Taylor W. Gannett
Taylor W. Gannett,
Vice Consul .... of the United
States of America.

CONSUL'S FINDINGS ON STATUS. (Include statements regarding evidence presented that alien has a fixed domicile and that he has a right to be readmitted into the country in which he is applying or into some other country.)

Applicant is going to reside in Georgetown, British Guiana where his brother is domiciled. Has permission to enter this country.

Passport visa granted ....August 7,....
1940...., as nonimmigrant under section 3 (3) of the Immigration Act of 1924.

Passport visa refused ....

19..   Reasons .....Orange......

Admitted at New York, N. Y.
AUG 2 0 1940
.....49...., under Paragraph 3 Section 3, Immigration Act of 1924.

A. C. Brown

H. Oxxxxd
Immigrant Inspector.

had Stock issue fire about 8/13/40

TRANSIT CERTIFICATE
(Issued in accordance with Executive Order of August 20, 1930)

No.................... American Consulate
at _Lisbon, Portugal_

I hereby certify that the bearer of this passport, according to satisfactory evidence produced to me, is about to pass through territory of the United States.
in transit to _British Guiana_
at (port of entry) _New York_
date of entry) _on or about August 18, 1940_
and (port of departure) _New York_
(date of departure) _on or about August 23, 1940_

Taylor Gannett
(seal)   Vice Consul
No Fee Prescribed

August 7 1940
(date)

U.S. GOVERNMENT PRINTING OFFICE   10—11203

Figure 1-6 The passport visa and attached Transit Certificate that allowed us to travel from Lisbon to New York.

Fortuitously, a ship bound for New York City was scheduled to leave Lisbon in a few days. Cabin space was available, but only in the least desirable (steerage) section of the ship. My father made the reservations without hesitation and then attempted to sell our De Soto. He quickly discovered that the municipality of Lisbon had passed a law forbidding the sale of cars belonging to non-Portuguese refugees. The sale of these cars provided useful revenue for the city. Eventually, he left the car on a street with the keys in the ignition. I could never understand why he did not keep the keys, or throw them away. Perhaps he was so grateful for the opportunity to leave Europe with his family unharmed that he felt the loss of the car was a small price to pay. Although it was commonly known that spies working for the German government had infiltrated Lisbon and some of the consulates, this surveillance fortunately did not affect the ability of my father to obtain a passport visa.

Our voyage across the Atlantic was uneventful. My father spent the entire time sitting on deck, because his tendency for seasickness made it difficult for him to tolerate our accommodations in steerage. A major concern, German submarines, did not apply to us because Portugal had declared itself neutral, and the inclination of the Portuguese government to favor Nazi Germany made an attack unlikely. We arrived in New York about ten days later in mid-August 1940.

Chapter 2

Life in Georgetown, British Guiana

ALTHOUGH OUR PASSPORT visa, with its attached Transit Certificate (fig. 1-6), permitted us to avoid Ellis Island, we still needed a place to stay temporarily, because our Transit Certificate did not permit permanent residence in the United States. Fortunately, my father knew of a distant relative living in the Seagate section of Brooklyn, who was willing to vouch for us and provide shelter, while my father attempted to contact his brother David in British Guiana. He was successful and obtained an affidavit that allowed us to enter and remain in the British colony.

Figure 2-1 The Victoria Law Courts in Georgetown.

Figure 2-2 The Town Hall in Georgetown.

Figure 2-3 The Stabroek Market in Georgetown. This market is an example of Dutch influence on architecture in Georgetown. From: *Guyana: In Pictures, Visual Geography Series,* (Lerner Publications Co.: Minneapolis, MN, 1988) p. 27.

I remember very little of our sea voyage from New York to Georgetown, the capital of British Guiana, but I have a vivid memory of seeing my uncle David, aunt Celly, and my two younger cousins, Isidore (Zizi) and Molly, waiting on the dock for us. Georgetown, while small in comparison with Antwerp and comparable European cities, did have a number of memorable buildings, including the Victoria Law Courts (fig. 2-1), Town Hall (fig. 2-2), and Stabroek Market (fig. 2-3). The architecture of these and other public buildings in Georgetown reflected a Dutch heritage, because British Guiana was intermittently under Dutch and British control during the eighteenth and nineteenth centuries; it became wholly British in 1831 under agreements contained in the Treaty of Paris and the Congress of Vienna. After a difficult period during the first half of the twentieth century, British Guiana finally achieved independence in 1966 and chose the name Guyana.

Life in Georgetown was initially a shock. We had been transported from a temperate to a tropical climate, and while my sister and I spoke

French and some Flemish, we spoke no English. The vegetation, such as the large star apple tree that grew outside the windows of the boarding house in which we initially lived, was strange. My sister and I were placed in a small private school that consisted of a room in a house run by a kind elderly teacher, whose main tasks were to protect me from the taunts of some of my classmates, and to teach us English as quickly as possible.

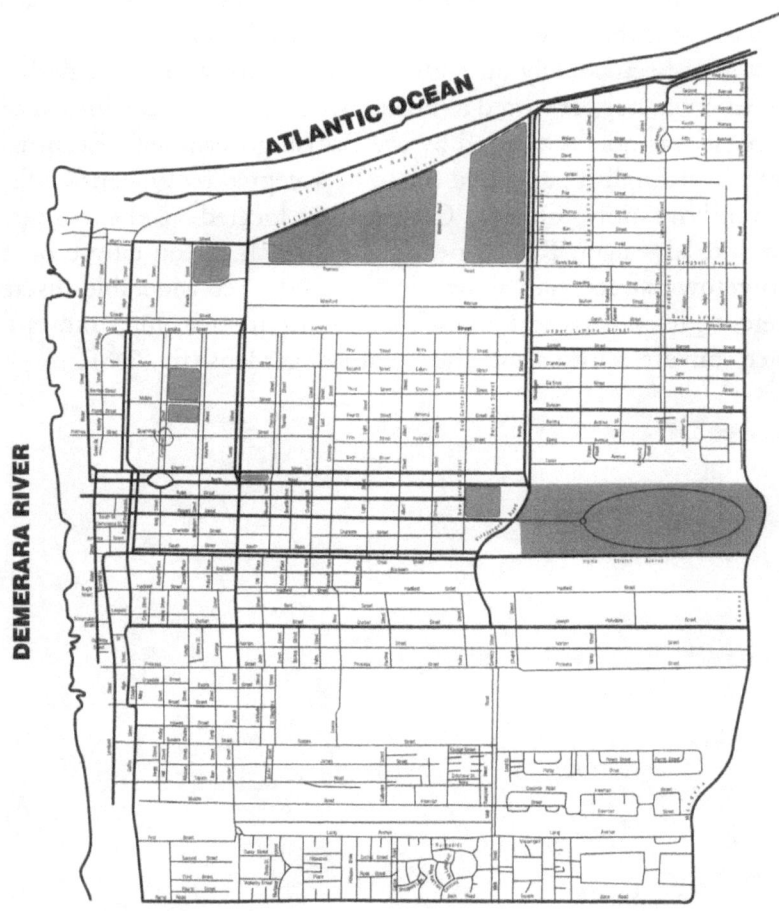

Figure 2-4 A street map of Georgetown, British Guiana. Google maps—@2012 Google, 1/31/12, 5:30 PM MST.

After some time in the boarding house, my parents rented a small house on Lamaha Street (see map, fig. 2-4), which had the advantage of being closer to the seashore, with its seawall and beach. However, we quickly became disenchanted with the beach, which bore little resemblance to the fine sand beach of the Belgian seashore to which we had become accustomed. In contrast, the beach consisted of mud, brought to the British Guiana seashore by the Amazon River to the east, and by other large rivers to the west. The British Guiana sand did, however, have one unique advantage. When scooped up by hand in the form of a pear and allowed to dry for a short time, it became a painful missile in "wars" between small groups of boys. It was not always easy to avoid these "wars," as I remember to this day.

It must have been equally difficult for my parents, and particularly for my father, who was not permitted to practice medicine because, initially, his Belgian license was not recognized by the British government. Eventually, my command of English permitted me to be accepted by Queens College, a school for boys only. Queens College was located at the corner of Brickdam and Vissengen Roads, near the racetrack (green ellipse on the early Georgetown street map shown in fig. 2-5), a considerable distance from where we lived. It is of interest that a current street map shows this green space converted into a zoo and botanical gardens (fig. 2-6).

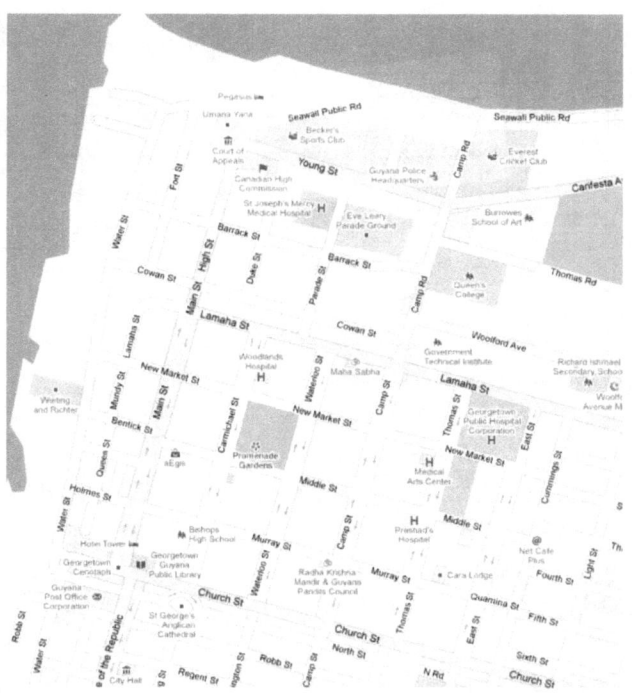

Figure 2-5 An early Georgetown street map (source unknown).

Figure 2-6 A current Georgetown street map showing that the previously described green space had been converted into a zoo and a botanical garden. Google Maps-@2012 Google, 1/31/12. 5:30 PM MST.

Since my parents did not own a car, I was obliged to learn to ride a bicycle, and to ride it on the left side of the road. Apparently, I acquired these skills rather easily; the light traffic during those war years was helpful.

Discipline at Queens College was strict. The headmaster was Captain Nobbs, presumably a retired military officer. Misbehavior in the classroom was not tolerated, and if repeated, was punished by a visit of the boy to

Captain Nobbs's office, whereupon the guilty boy was invited to touch his toes in order to receive lashes with a cane on his bottom, the number depending on the seriousness of his infraction. The system was primitive, but effective, and did not interfere with learning. When I arrived in the United States in 1947 at the age of thirteen, I was given a comprehensive exam and, based on the results, was placed in the tenth grade. Fortunately, my father had the common sense to delay my graduation from high school and my entry into college by a year.

Figure 2-7 A photograph of my sister, Viviane, as a student at Bishop's High School for girls.

My sister (fig. 2-7) was admitted to Bishops High School for girls, located at Carmichael Street (fig. 2-4), shortly after our family moved to Vreed en Hoop. After taking the ferry across the Demerara River, she passed through the Stabroek Market on her bicycle, headed up Water Street, and cut across Church Street to reach her school. Occasionally, she would stop in the public library on Church Street (fig. 2-4). She remembers, particularly, the lobby exhibit of Amerindians, with a canoe, who lived in the interior of British Guiana. She also recalls visiting St. George's cathedral nearby, a tall and imposing wood structure with a beautiful interior.

Bishops High School was typically British in having a very thorough and demanding curriculum. As my sister recalls, she started with algebra and geometry, as well as with French and Latin, at the age of ten. She was also taught about the British Empire and thereby gained a good grasp of world geography. In indoor gym classes, one of the activities entailed walking on balance beams with books on the students' heads to improve their posture. My sister recalls that a particularly strict teacher harshly berated her for squinting when she was trying to read something on the blackboard. It was an embarrassing incident. At the time, she was unaware that she was very nearsighted in one eye.

Figure 2-8 A photograph of our cousins with my sister and me; from *left to right*: Molly, Paul, Zizi, and Viviane.

Figure 2-9 A photograph, at an earlier date; *left to right*: Aunt Celly, Uncle David, my mother and father, and *below,* Viviane and I.

While we lived in Georgetown, my sister and I often played with our cousin, Zizi. His sister, Molly, was too young to participate at the time (fig. 2-8). Similarly, our parents socialized frequently (fig. 2-9). Uncle David was in the diamond trade, in partnership with two other uncles, Henry, with whom we drove from Antwerp to Bordeaux (see Chapter 1), and William, who had left Antwerp with his family for Palestine in 1936. The three uncles had taken turns in running the business in British Guiana, but the war had disrupted this schedule.

After we moved to Vreed en Hoop (see Chapter 3), our contacts were less frequent. This change was not only the consequence of the need to take the ferry, but also because my father was reluctant to take the admittedly small risk that his nephew or niece might be exposed to tuberculosis, a danger that was a consequence of his new employment.

Chapter 3

The Move from Georgetown to Vreed en Hoop, British Guiana

IN 1943, A change of policy by the British government made it possible for my father to practice medicine in British Guiana. Because of the increasing scope of World War II and a shortage of physicians trained in the British Isles, the requirement that only British-trained physicians could practice medicine in British colonies was lifted. Permission was granted for practice by physicians whose training and license were obtained in countries in which the standard of medical education was considered comparable to that in Britain. Fortunately, that requirement was easily satisfied by my father's credentials, obtained in Belgium and Switzerland. As a physician who contracted tuberculosis, probably as a medical student or intern while working in hospitals in Brussels, my father went to the tuberculosis sanatorium in Davos, Switzerland, with the rather faint hope of a cure. Davos, because of its high altitude and low oxygen tension, was known to be a favorable place for patients to live, because the tubercle bacillus requires oxygen to survive and proliferate, and effective antibiotics were not available at that time. It turned out that my father's infection was not only arrested, but that he also became immune to subsequent reinfection. While in Davos, my father also learned the procedure for pneumothorax (indeed he underwent the procedure himself)—the collapse of a lung by the introduction of a large needle through the chest wall. In effect, this procedure starves the lung of oxygen and prevents further growth of the tubercle bacillus. If kept at bed rest, an individual can survive easily, breathing with only one lung.

Fortuitously, the Best Tuberculosis Sanatorium, located in a sparsely-populated section of Vreed en Hoop, a village on the other side of the Demerara River from Georgetown, was in need of a medical superintendent. Presumably, the post was not a very popular one, but it was a perfect fit for my father. On June 4, 1943, my father was appointed medical superintendent of the Vreed en Hoop Best Tuberculosis Sanatorium (fig. 3-1). Previously he had been certified to be free of active tuberculosis (fig. 3-2), an obvious requirement for the position.

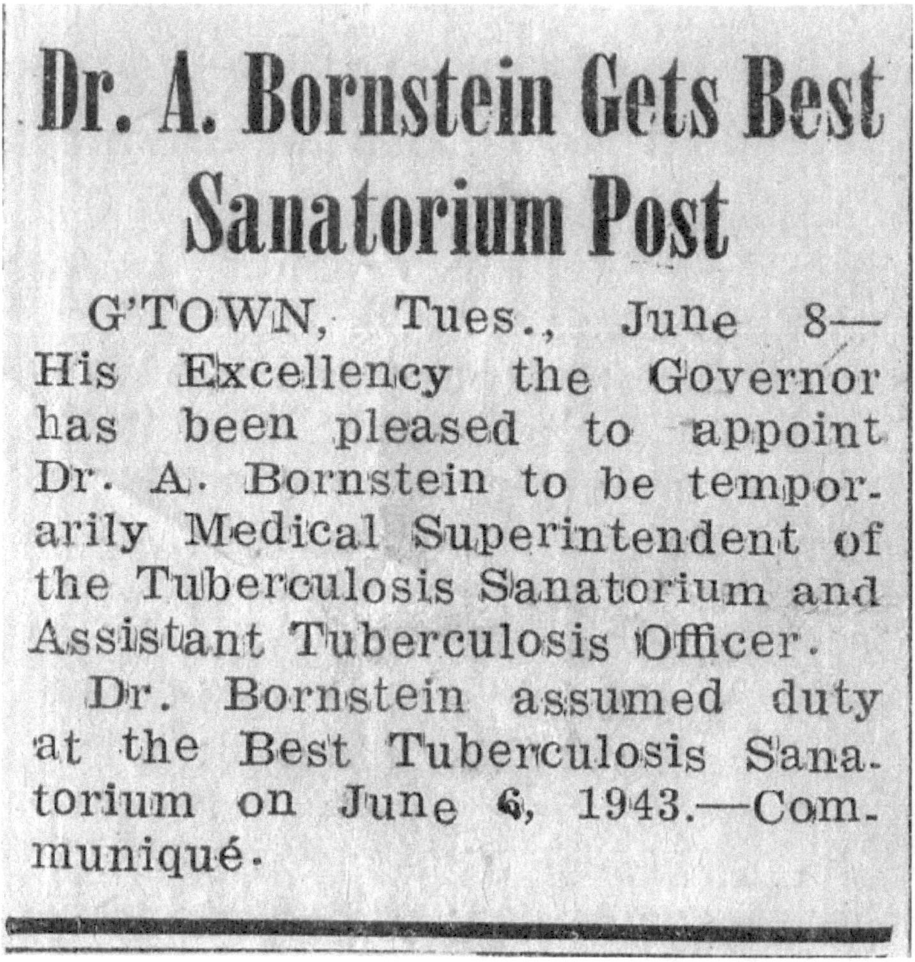

Dr. A. Bornstein Gets Best Sanatorium Post

G'TOWN, Tues., June 8— His Excellency the Governor has been pleased to appoint Dr. A. Bornstein to be temporarily Medical Superintendent of the Tuberculosis Sanatorium and Assistant Tuberculosis Officer.

Dr. Bornstein assumed duty at the Best Tuberculosis Sanatorium on June 6, 1943.—Communiqué.

Figure 3-1 The announcement, clipped by my mother from a local Georgetown newspaper, of the appointment of my father to the post of medical superintendent of the Tuberculosis Sanatorium. My mother was an avid monitor of my father's professional career.

COPY

Eve Leary Barracks,
Georgetown,
British Guiana.
11th January, 1943.

To: W.S. Jones Esq.
Hony. Consul for Belgium,
British Guiana.

Sir,

I have today medically examined Dr A. Bornstein, now residing at 3 High Street Georgetown, with a view to pronouncing on his fitness for Military Service.

He gives a history and documentary evidence of having suffered from Tuberculosis, primary attack in 1935, under treatment till August 1939, pneumothorax in January 1936. Since 1939 he has had no symptoms except that he feels he becomes quickly tired and run down and develops a short cough after exertion.

Otherwise his medical history and family history are good.

On examination, no evidence of any active lesion in the lungs can be detected, the sounds being almost normal.

There is slight enlargement of the heart towards the right and some tachy cardia pulse 96.

No abnormalities of the other systems were detected.

In view of his tubercular history, I do not consider Dr. Bornstein fit for active military service. As the disease has been quiescent for two years; he could be placed in grade 111, fit for sedentary work at a garrison or base in a hospital or office.

(Sgd) J.W. Thomson,
Surgeon Captain,
B.G. Militia.

I hereby certify the above to be a true copy.

HONY. CONSUL FOR BELGIUM
Georgetown, British Guiana.

Figure 3-2 A certification that my father was free of active tuberculosis was an obvious requirement for the position of medical superintendent.

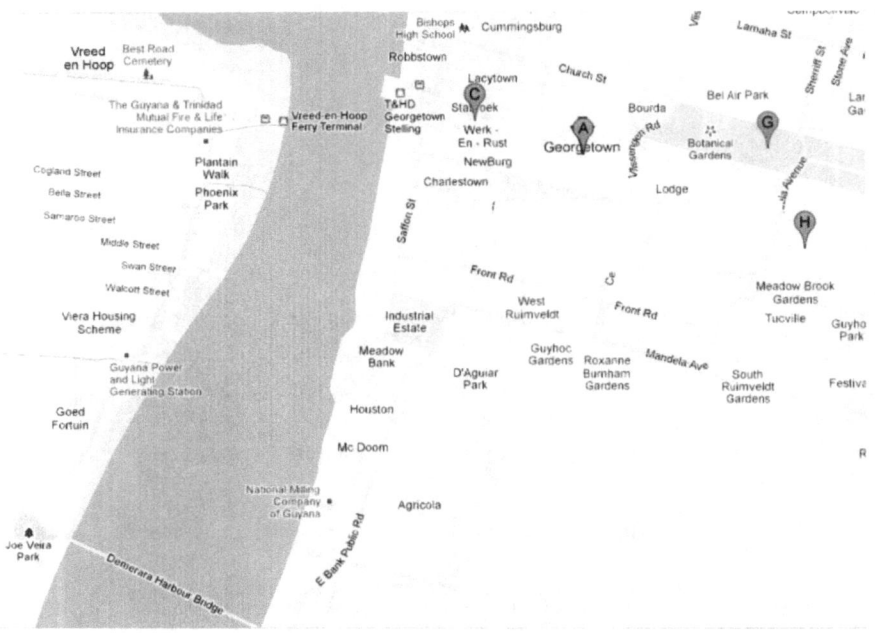

Figure 3-3 A new bridge was built across the Demerara River, from Vreed en Hoop to the East Bank public road, south of Georgetown. Google Maps-@ 2012 Google, 1/31/12, 5:30 PM MST.

When we moved to Vreed en Hoop (Dutch for faith and hope) in 1943, the only buildings of any consequence were those that comprised the Best Tuberculosis Sanatorium and an Anglican church located near the ferry dock. It would be misleading to show a current map of Vreed en Hoop, because the village today features several large hotels and many other structures that did not exist in 1943. Growth was undoubtedly spurred by the construction of a bridge across the Demerara River, a short distance south of Georgetown (fig. 3-3). Prior to the building of the bridge, all traffic across the river was by a ferry, which ran from a point near the Atlantic Ocean in Vreed en Hoop, to a wharf close to the Stabroek Market in Georgetown. Communities such as Schoonord and Lagrange, shown in figure 3-4, did not exist or were not named; at least not to my knowledge, when we lived in Vreed en Hoop. The road along the Atlantic Ocean ran west to end at Parika on the border of the Essequibo River. The Best Sanatorium was located close to the Atlantic Ocean at the point where the road to Parika turns north.

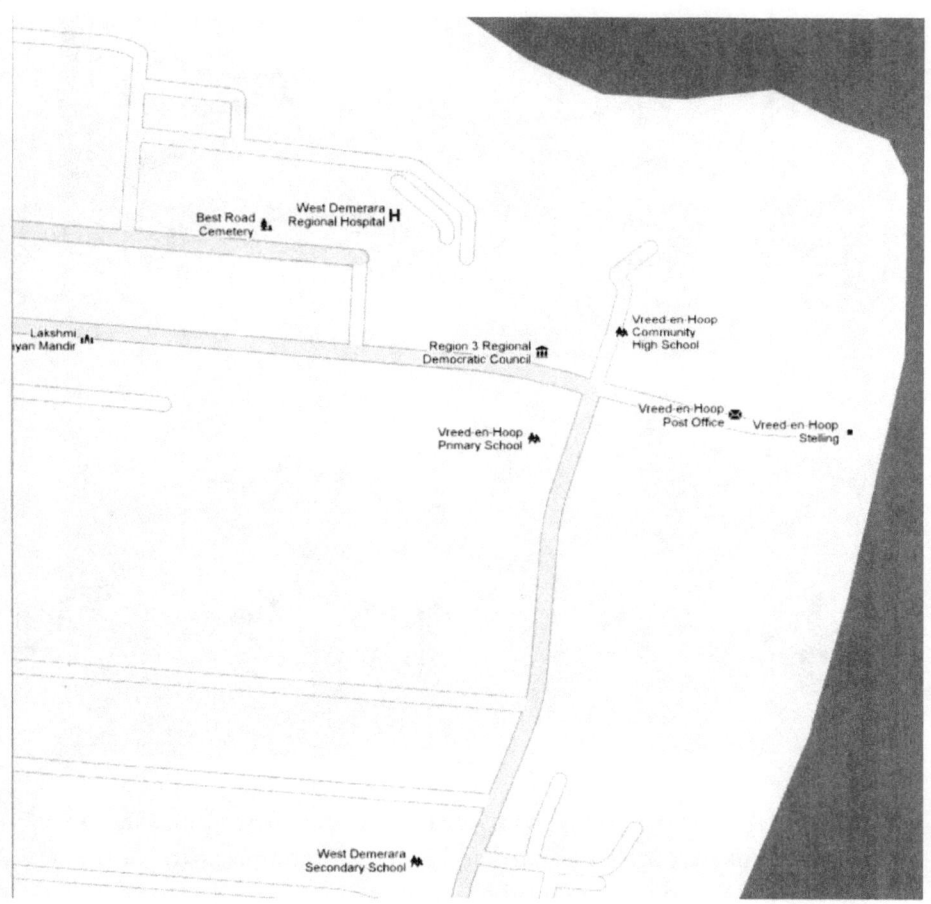

Figure 3-4 The new bridge spurs growth of Vreed en Hoop and reduces the need for a ferry across the river. Google Maps-@ 2012 Google, 1/31/12, 5:30 PM MST.

Settling in on the grounds of the Best Tuberculosis Sanatorium in Vreed en Hoop and going to school in Georgetown

Figure 3-5 The various components of the Best Tuberculosis Sanatorium are widely separated and isolated from other parts of the compound to reduce the spread of the disease.

As shown in figure 3-5, the various components of the Best Tuberculosis Sanatorium were widely separated and isolated from other parts of the compound to avoid contact of potentially infectious patients with the support staff who worked in the kitchen, pharmacy, laundry, and other places. Our family was housed in a small apartment above the pharmacy, which was located near the exit gate of the compound. My sister and I were warned not to wander near the hospital buildings, a warning that we respected; and not to climb on the natural rock jetties that separated the Atlantic Ocean from the Demerara River, a temptation that we could not resist. It was only much later that we learned that the turbulence we saw in the water, which we thought was due to many small fish, was actually made by poisonous sea snakes of the deadliest variety.

To access the road that led to the ferry, a distance of about a mile, we first crossed an irrigation stream and a railroad. The road itself was not paved, but there were two parallel concrete strips that allowed a car or truck to avoid the mud and potholes of the dirt road. The concrete strips were warmed by the sun during the day, and proved to be attractive places for the ubiquitous snakes that inhabited the adjacent woods to keep themselves warm during the cool of the night. From time to time, a car or truck would drive on the concrete strips early in the morning and crush a large number and assortment of snakes, leaving many of them still writhing and only half-dead. To pass such a scene on bicycle proved to be a daunting and truly frightening experience for a young boy, who had already been warned of the dangers of poisonous snakes in British Guiana. My sister, who rode her bicycle to school at a different time, reported a somewhat similar experience with a cayman, which seemed very much alive. Perhaps these experiences inured us to the dangers of crossing city streets that we experienced later in Brooklyn. While the ride across the Demerara River was generally a sleepy experience, I was jarred awake one morning when a large freighter rammed our ferry and produced a hole in its hull (fortunately above the waterline). This incident caused momentary panic among the passengers—I don't believe that the ferry carried lifeboats. When I was asked by my parents what I did at that time, I confessed that I ran below to secure my new bicycle that I had received from my Uncle David. After the end of the war in 1945, it was safe for boats to travel to Georgetown with nonessential cargo. I was roundly criticized by my parents, who pointed out that I couldn't swim carrying my bicycle; in any case, I couldn't swim at all at that time.

The staff at the Best Sanatorium

Perhaps because of its isolation, and because a large majority of the staff lived on or near the grounds of the hospital, the relationship of members of the staff to each other seemed to be closer than those that might be expected in a typical urban hospital in the United States. Close social interactions, regardless of rank, were also promoted by my father, who seemed to have an ability to make each member of the staff feel that all individuals were essential, as indeed they were. A photograph (fig. 3-6; date unknown) of some of the staff reflects this attitude. The individuals are identified on the back of the photograph as follows:

Figure 3-6 Some of the staff at the Best Sanatorium. The identities of the individuals are described in the text.

Front row: A. Pakeman (matron, probably a senior nurse); my father; W. R. Cummings (steward)

Middle row: U. E. Parks (clerk); R. Tawari (lab. technician); Dr. B. B. G. Nehaul (visiting government bacteriologist and pathologist); D. E. Wharton (dispenser/ pharmacist)

Back Row: R. G. Singh (electrician); K. Baksh (chauffeur).

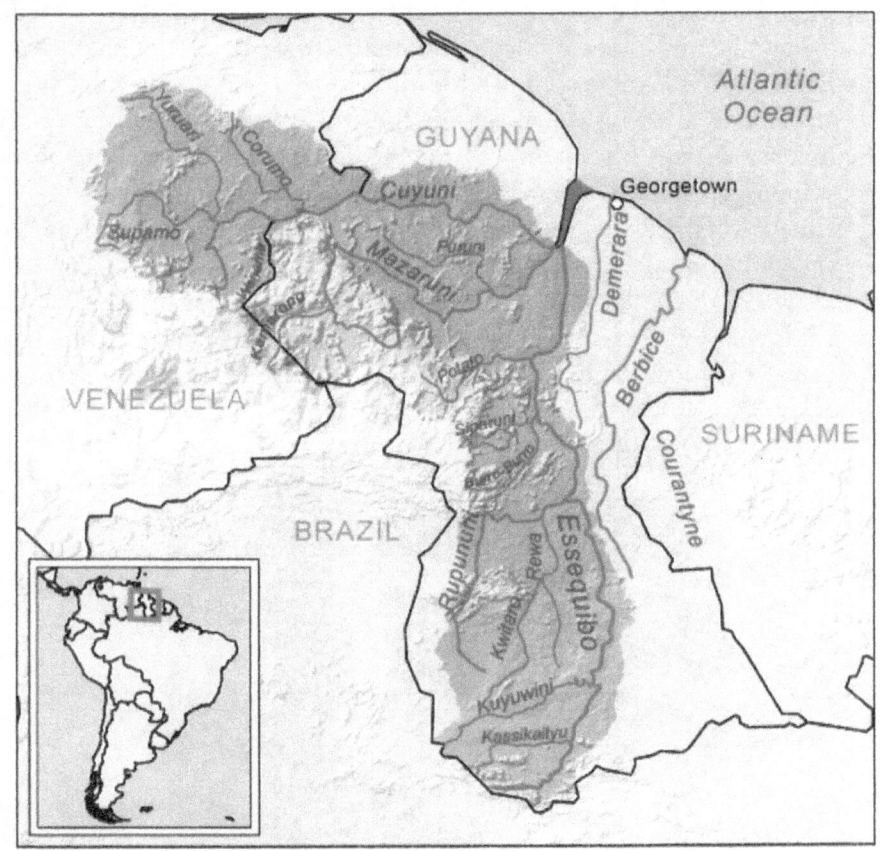

Figure 3-7 The village of Bartica is at the confluence of the Essequibo, Cuyuni-Mazaruni and Potaro Rivers. http://en.wikipedia.org/wiki/File:Essequiborivermap.png.

As an official of the British Guiana Department of Health, my father was asked to visit various clinical outposts throughout the country, mainly along its rivers and seacoast, because the interior of the country was still dangerous and difficult to reach. On occasion he would take me, or my sister and me, along. My favorite voyage was to Bartica, then a small village but now a small town at the confluence of the Essequibo, Cuyuni-Mazaruni, and Potaro Rivers (fig. 3-7). Our voyage started in Georgetown, where we boarded a relatively large ferry that entered the Atlantic Ocean and traveled west to the Essequibo River. Predictably, because of his propensity for seasickness, my father found a deck chair and lay in it for the entire voyage, even though the water was quite calm. As we entered the mouth of the Essequibo, and sailed along its right bank, I saw some relatively low-lying mountains, the first mountains I could remember seeing; I still remember the thrill of that sight. My fascination with mountains lasted for the rest of my life and led many years later to my climbing, together with some highly experienced mountaineers, some of the highest mountains in the state of Washington in the USA.

While my father was busy in the clinic in Bartica, my sister and I, together with a guide, enjoyed bathing in some wonderfully cool pools, formed by the rivers that converged on the village. Part of my fascination with the pools resulted from my being told that the Kaieteur Falls (fig. 3-8), one of the most famous natural wonders in British Guiana, was in the path of the Potaro River.

Figure 3-8 The Kaieteur Falls on the Potaro River is the world's highest single-drop waterfall. At a height of 741 feet, it is three times higher than Niagara Falls. http://en.wikipedia.org/wiki/File:GuyanaKaieteurFalls2004.jpg.

Our family increased in size by the birth of my brother

My brother, Isaac, was born on June 20, 1945; nearly five years after our family had arrived in British Guiana. To this day, I cannot remember any signs of pregnancy in my mother. I do remember on the day of his birth that I was told to go outside and not to come back until I was asked to do so, a command which I thought was unusual. My father delivered my brother by himself, with the sole assistance of a nurse. In retrospect, as a physician, I find this unusual since his last experience as a gynecologist must have been ten years earlier, while he was an intern in Brussels. A photograph of our family, taken in November 1945, is shown in figure 3-9.

Figure 3-9 A photograph of our family, with its youngest member Isaac, taken in November 1945.

Chapter 4

A Decision Not to Return to Belgium in Favor of Emigration to the United States

IN 1946, AFTER matters began to return to normal in Europe, my father traveled to Belgium via New York, to determine whether it was feasible for our family to return to Antwerp. I was not privy to the discussions that my parents had on this question, but as time passed, it became evident that both my parents, but particularly my father, were reluctant to return to a country that, while not supporting the Nazi occupation, did little to resist it. The decision not to return to Belgium was courageous in that the alternative, which was clearly to go to the United States, required passing of the medical board examinations and becoming familiar with a rather different social and medical culture. As I learned later, the decision not to return to Antwerp was also made despite the assurance of several of my father's former colleagues that there was ample opportunity to restart a successful medical practice in Belgium.

While in Antwerp, my father had an opportunity to visit the house he abandoned in 1940. He was told by neighbors that German officers had used the house as a type of headquarters during the war. Although it was in good condition, the house was completely empty with the exception of the Bechstein baby grand piano and a crystal chandelier. He sold the piano and brought the chandelier back with him. Eventually the chandelier hung in his retirement home and now rests in the apartment of a granddaughter.

A holiday in Barbados prior to leaving British Guiana

During the Easter holidays in 1947, my parents, perhaps sensing the growing anxiety in my sister and me, arranged for our mother and all three children to go on a brief holiday in Barbados, a Caribbean Island close to British Guiana known for its beautiful beaches. Travel was to be by airplane, a mode of transportation that none of us, including my father, had experienced. For reasons that remain unclear, my sister and I were to leave a day before my mother and brother. We arrived without incident and were met at the airport by personnel from the hotel as planned. However, on the following day, when our mother and brother were scheduled to arrive, we were told that they would be delayed by a few days and that we would be under the supervision of the hotel staff until they arrived. It developed that my mother became afraid of flying and decided to leave the flight at an intermediate stop in Trinidad, and to continue to Barbados by boat. As I recall, my sister and I took full advantage of the loose supervision by the hotel staff until my mother arrived. During our remaining time in Barbados, we all enjoyed the warm weather and beautiful sand beaches, which were in striking contrast to the unpleasant Georgetown seashore.

An unexpected early departure by boat for the United States

Our return to Georgetown by boat was uneventful, as was the start of school, but in early May, my father was informed with very little notice that passage by boat to the United States, specifically to Mobile, Alabama, was available. My sister and I were suddenly obliged to stop attending school, without even saying goodbye to our classmates, an event that I regretted for many years. Passage was by freighter carrying bauxite for the Alcoa Company. The ship had a single cabin for passengers that we were fortunate to occupy, and made intermediate stops in Dutch Guiana and Trinidad that added to the excitement of the voyage for my sister and me. Some of the subsequent boredom of the voyage was dispelled after I was able to make friends with the captain, who seemed to have little to do once the ship was in open water. We both loved to play chess and we were about evenly matched, in contrast to my father, who taught me how to play the game but was reluctant to play once I started to win regularly. For variety, the captain quizzed me on the names of the capital cities of states in the USA, a game at which I failed miserably. How could New York City not be the capital of New York State, and who ever heard of Albany? Fortunately, I was able to get Boston and Massachusetts right!

From Mobile, Alabama, to Brooklyn, New York, by train and the end of our seven-year journey from Antwerp to New York

This final stage of our trip was exciting for me because I did not recall ever having traveled on a high-speed train. Surprisingly, I do not remember very much about the trip. I may have been preoccupied by what I should do about the large safari-like helmet that I wore. I had noticed that no one I saw wore a hat like mine, and that I was attracting curious glances. I therefore devised a plan to get rid of the helmet. As we were leaving the train, I simply placed the helmet on my seat and left the train without it. By the time my mother noticed that I no longer had the helmet, it was too late to retrieve it. She was furious, of course, but she was too concerned with finding the distant relative who was to guide us to Brooklyn and find a place for us to stay, to continue to berate me.

Our initial stay in Brooklyn was rather chaotic and challenging, at least for me. My mother, sister, and brother found a small apartment in the Brighton Beach district, whereas I slept on a couch in the living room of a former American Air Force officer whom my father had befriended in British Guiana during the war. This placed me within walking distance of Tilden High School, although the heavy traffic, traffic signals, and police and fire truck sirens were disconcerting and confusing to a young boy whose city experience had been rather minimal. School posed a different challenge, because I was constantly mocked by my classmates on account of my Caribbean accent and short pants. Pleading with my mother for long pants solved the latter problem, whereas the former faded with time.

Epilogue

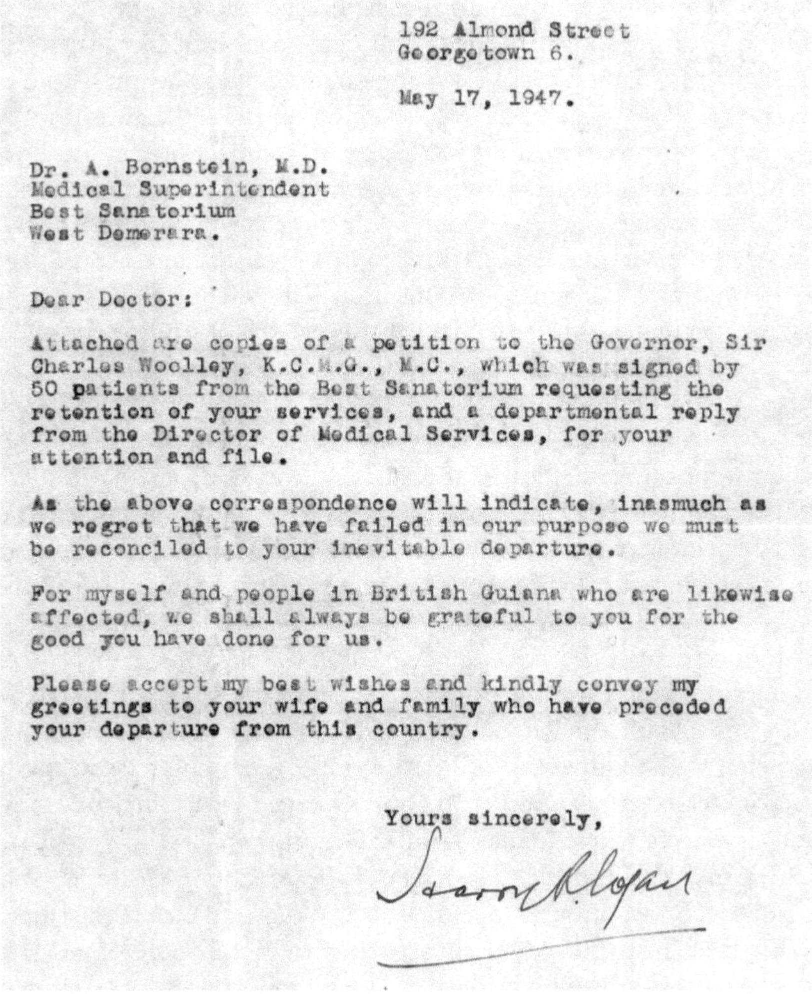

192 Almond Street
Georgetown 6.

May 17, 1947.

Dr. A. Bornstein, M.D.
Medical Superintendent
Best Sanatorium
West Demerara.

Dear Doctor:

Attached are copies of a petition to the Governor, Sir
Charles Woolley, K.C.M.G., M.C., which was signed by
50 patients from the Best Sanatorium requesting the
retention of your services, and a departmental reply
from the Director of Medical Services, for your
attention and file.

As the above correspondence will indicate, inasmuch as
we regret that we have failed in our purpose we must
be reconciled to your inevitable departure.

For myself and people in British Guiana who are likewise
affected, we shall always be grateful to you for the
good you have done for us.

Please accept my best wishes and kindly convey my
greetings to your wife and family who have preceded
your departure from this country.

Yours sincerely,

[signature]

Figure 4-1 A petition to the governor of British Guiana, signed by fifty former patients of the Best Sanatorium, requesting retention of my father's services after he had announced his intention to leave the country.

M Y FATHER JOINED us a few months after we had rented a small house in the Coney Island section of Brooklyn. He received many letters from former patients attesting to his skill as a physician and thanking him for the care he had given them. A petition, signed by fifty former patients of the Best Sanatorium, requesting retention of my father's services was submitted to the governor of British Guiana (fig. 4-1). With the advent of antibiotics, a Sanatorium dedicated solely to the treatment of tuberculosis was no longer needed. The Best Sanatorium was accordingly remodeled and renamed the West Demerara Regional Hospital. To qualify for the practice of medicine in New York State, my father was obliged to serve as an intern for a year and to pass a rigorous examination, both of which he performed satisfactorily. After serving for a year as a pulmonologist at King's County Hospital in Brooklyn, my father opened a private practice in Brooklyn that he maintained until my parents retired to San Diego in 1977. However, he continued to consult at King's County Hospital while in Brooklyn. He died of Alzheimer's disease at the age of ninety-one. My mother survived him and lived to the age of ninety-five.

After attending three different high schools in three years in Brooklyn, I graduated from Cornell University with a major in chemistry in 1954 and then went on to medical school at New York University, from which I graduated with an MD degree in 1958. After a disappointing experience as a surgical intern at Yale University School of Medicine, I completed a medical residency at Yale and spent a year at the Pasteur Institute in Paris on an Arthritis Foundation Fellowship. With the war in Vietnam in progress, I was inducted into the coast guard, but I was fortunate to be able to spend almost all my time performing biochemical research at the National Institutes of Health. In 1967, I accepted a position as assistant professor of medicine at the University of Washington. As my interests in the basic sciences increased, my appointment was changed to a joint appointment in biochemistry and medicine. With the exception of sabbatical years at the University of California, San Diego, in 1975; the Institute de Chemie Biologique in Strasbourg, France, in 1985; a Guggenheim fellowship, and the Whitehead Institute, Massachusetts Institute of Technology (MIT) in 1991, I remained at the University of Washington until my retirement as professor emeritus of biochemistry and medicine in 2007. I now live in New Mexico.

My sister, Viviane, was salutatorian of the 1952 graduating class at New Utrecht High School in Brooklyn. She attended Barnard College, majored in chemistry and worked for six years as a technical writer for the Air Reduction Chemical Company in New York City. In 1958, she married Jonas Schultz, a Columbia College graduate with a major in physics. They moved to Berkeley, California, in 1963 for his postdoctoral research at the university there. His 1966 professorial appointment at the University of California, Irvine, brought them to Southern California, where they raised their three children and continue to live today. Starting in 1980, Viviane had a second career as a faculty housing administrator at UC Irvine for more than twenty years.

My brother, Isaac, graduated from MIT with a BS degree in physics in 1966. He graduated from the University of California, Berkeley with an MS in nuclear engineering in 1968, as well as an MS in electrical engineering and computer science and a PhD in nuclear engineering in 1971. He worked for the Naval Undersea Research and Development Center (later called the Naval Undersea Center) in Pasadena and San Diego, California, from 1971 to 1978 and subsequently changed to medicine. He received the MD degree from the University of California, San Diego Medical School, in 1982 and trained in radiology at the Mayo Clinic in Rochester, Minnesota. He is currently a radiologist in Bakersfield, California.

Not long before he died, I visited my father in San Diego. It was clear that he was in the late stages of Alzheimer's disease. He was seriously confused and had difficulty in speaking and walking. Nevertheless, my mother thought he might profit from a short walk. I therefore took him to a nearby park. My father was silent as we left his house and walked with a slow shuffling gait. As we approached the first bench, he appeared exhausted, so we both sat down. He looked away for quite some time. Suddenly he turned toward me and said in a clear voice, "You know, Paul, we didn't do so bad." I was startled but I responded, "Yes, Dad, thanks to you we didn't do so bad." I thought I saw a slight smile cross his face before he turned away and sank once again into silence.

Acknowledgments

I AM INDEBTED TO my wife, Dr. Helene Sage, for encouraging me to write this book, and for a careful proofreading of this manuscript. I thank my sister, Viviane Schultz, for preserving most of the documents used in this book and for contributing her recollection of some of the incidents described in it, all of which improved its authenticity. I am also grateful to Dr. Jonas Schultz for additional proofreading, and for assistance with retrieving information from the Internet.

INDEX

Treaty of Paris, 18
tuberculosis, 12, 25–27, 30, 40

U

United States, 14, 22, 36–37

V

Vreed en Hoop, 22, 24, 28–29
   moving to, 25

W

West Demerara Regional Hospital,
   40. *See also* Best Tuberculosis
   Sanatorium
William (Paul's uncle), 24
World War II, 25